Craft Sale

Earn money making
and selling fun and
easy crafts

CRAFT
sale
today!

handmade

by Megan,
Carrie, and
Lindsey

★ American Girl®

Published by American Girl Publishing, Inc.

Copyright © 2008 by American Girl, LLC

Questions or comments? Call 1-800-845-0005,
visit our Web site at **americangirl.com**,
or write to Customer Service, American Girl,
8400 Fairway Place, Middleton, WI 53562-0497.

Printed in China

08 09 10 11 12 LEO 10 9 8 7 6 5 4 3 2

All American Girl marks are trademarks of American Girl, LLC.

Editorial Development: Carrie Anton, Jessica Hastreiter, Kristi Thom, Laura Torres, Michelle Watkins, Sarah Yates

Art Direction & Design: Camela Decaire, Julie Mierkiewicz, Lara Klipsch Elliott, Susan Casey, Ginkgo Creative

Production: Kendra Schluter, Gretchen Krause, Jeannette Bailey, Judith Lary, Barbara Stretchberry

Illustrations: Ali Douglass

Photography: Chris Hynes, Jim Jordan, Steven Talley, Mike Walker, Jamie Young, Radlund Photography

Stylists: Carrie Anton, Camela Decaire, Jessica Hastreiter, Julie Mierkiewicz

Special thanks to Katie B. for giving us a hand. And thank you to
Hanna, Lauren, and Sierra for making and selling the crafts.

Projects on pages 40, 41, 42, and 43 courtesy of Tulip® and Aleene's® for Duncan Enterprises.
For more information, call 1-800-438-6226.

Dear Reader,

Do you love to create things and want to earn some extra money? Then this book is for you! We've picked the best crafts from *American Girl* magazine that are easy to make and great to sell.

Follow the instructions to make the crafts. Then use the price tags, business cards, display pieces, stamp, and stickers in the kit to start you on the path to selling smart. The receipt pad and ledger will help you manage any money you make.

So . . . get ready, craft, sell!

Your friends at American Girl

Table of Contents

Business Basics

Spring Craft Show

Summer Stand

Fall Festival

Winter Bazaar

Starting Up

Starting tips to make your craft sale a super success!

Where will you sell your crafts?

The first step is to find a place to set up your sale.

- If a local church or community center is having a summer craft show or holiday bazaar, ask a parent to help you find out how to set up a table to sell your crafts.

- Have a sale at your house. Ask your parents if you can invite friends and neighbors to an inside sale or set up a stand outside.

- Ask your principal if your school can have a craft fair. Or if you have a school store, ask if you can sell some crafts there.

My Booth!

HANDMADE Magnets & Bracelets!

When will you have your sale?

Think of a good time to hold your sale. If you'll be selling at an event such as a church craft sale, then your date is already set. But if you're selling solo, you'll need to pick a date and time.

Weekends are better than weekdays. Pick a time when lots of people are likely to be out, and let a parent know what you're planning. If you set up a stand during a neighborhood-wide garage sale or garden walk, you'll have plenty of customers.

How much time do you have?

Be sure to give yourself enough time. Working on your crafts over a week or two is more fun than trying to make them all the night before.

Consider asking a friend for help. Decide which crafts you'll make. Then split the cost of the supplies, split the work, and split the profits, too!

Get Crafty

Be as creative as you can be with your crafts!

Now that you know where to sell and when you'll be selling, it's time to figure out what to sell. Pick something that you'll enjoy making and that is appropriate for the season in which you're selling.

Read the directions carefully for each craft. The supplies you'll need to make each craft are listed in colored type. Before you begin, gather everything you'll need.

When working with glue or paint, be sure to cover your work area with newspaper.

Glues

Always use craft glue unless the directions list another kind. It works well because it cleans up easily with water.

Make it your own

The supplies listed for each craft will help you make what is pictured, but don't be afraid to give each craft your own personal touch. Change colors, add glitter—whatever! Just be creative.

Perfect Prices

Make sure the price is right to sell!

Prices for supplies vary from store to store. We've suggested prices for each craft throughout the book, but these tips will help you set the right price based on what you spent.

- Figure out what it costs to make one item. Add up the cost of all the materials you used to make each item.

- Whatever the cost of the materials, double that amount to get the minimum price you should ask.

- Make sure your prices are fair. If you ask too much, no one will buy your crafts. If you ask too little, you won't make a profit.

- Use the price tags in the kit (or make your own using the kit tags as a guide) to show customers how much each item costs.

Income

What I will charge for Garden Greetings packs of four cards plus envelopes
__$4__

In one month, I expect to sell __25__ packs

My TOTAL monthly income will be __$100__

Expenses

envelopes __$20__

paper __$14__

stickers __$8__

ribbon __$8__

My TOTAL monthly expenses __$50__

Profit

__$100__ — __$50__ = __$50__
my income   my expenses   my profit before taxes

Displays That Sell!

Use these ideas to show off your stuff.

- Don't just put your crafts in a pile when presenting them to customers. Organize your crafts on the table, and use the table tents in the kit to tell customers what you're selling and the price.

- Use the trifold table tents to display bobby pins, tacks, and magnets.

- Jazz up your table by covering it with a solid-colored tablecloth.

- Make a colorful sign calling attention to your table.

CRAFT
sale
today!

- Smile! A great grin will be sure to help you sell your crafts.

- There's no need to display your money! Keep your cash box tucked away for safekeeping.

- Leave a stack of business cards on your table so that customers can spread the word about your sale.

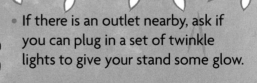

- If there is an outlet nearby, ask if you can plug in a set of twinkle lights to give your stand some glow.

- Show that your items are handmade by writing your name on the stickers in the kit or on a stamped piece of paper.

handmade by Megan, Carrie, and Lindsey.

Cash Care

Be smart with money matters.

Make change.
Before you start selling, have plenty of change so that you don't have to turn customers away. Start with 20 single bills and lots of coin change.

Keep track.
For each customer, write a receipt using the pad in your kit and record the sale in your ledger. Use this record to see how all of your crafts are selling.

Don't forget to donate.
If you want to help a good cause, pick a charity such as an animal shelter or a food bank to which to donate part of your profits. Let customers know that you'll be giving to charity so that they'll feel good about what they buy.

10% of PROFITS
DONATED to
Lakeview Animal Shelter

Safety First

Always play it safe when you sell.

When advertising and running your craft stand, be sure to follow these important safety tips.

- Include only your first name and a parent's e-mail address on business cards or flyers that you hand out or hang in public areas. Talk with your parents about safe places to do both. If you plan to go door-to-door with flyers or business cards, be sure to have an adult go with you.

- Always have a parent or trusted adult with you when selling crafts.

- If you're making lots of money at the craft stand in your front yard, bring some of the extra cash indoors for safekeeping.

-  Ask an adult! When you see this symbol, always ask an adult to help you.

Spring Craft Show

Customers go crazy for crafts when spring holidays such as Easter and Mother's Day arrive. These beautiful blossoms are sure to get your craft business booming!

Bitty Bobbies

For each bobby, you will need:
- 1 shank button
- 1 bobby pin

Slide a shank button (the kind with a loop on the back) onto a fancy bobby pin. Pin one or two into your hair when you're selling to show how cute they are.

Cost: $0.25
Price: $0.50
Profit: $0.25

Tip: *Clip the bobbies to a green trifold table tent to look like flowers growing out of the grass.*

Fuzzy Flowers

For each flower, you will need:
- 2 pieces of 3-foot-long yarn
- 1 pipe cleaner
- 1 pom-pom
- craft glue

1. Wrap the yarn around your fingers to create a loop as shown above.

2.  Pinch the yarn loop together and twist the pipe cleaner tightly around the center.

3. Pull yarn around to look like a flower. Glue a pom-pom in the center of the flower and let dry.

Cost: $0.50
Price: $1.00
Profit: $0.50

Tip: *Display in a small vase.*

Garden Greetings

You will need:
- 8.5-inch-by-11-inch patterned paper
- scissors
- flower stickers
- prepackaged envelopes
- ribbon

Cut an 8.5-inch-by-11-inch patterned paper in half. Fold each piece in half to create 2 cards. Decorate cards with flower stickers. Sell in packages of 4 cards and 4 envelopes (from office-supply and craft stores).

Tip: *Tie each package together with a pretty ribbon.*

Cost: $2.00
Price: $4.00
Profit: $2.00

Bookmark Blooms

You will need:
- scissors
- craft foam
- craft glue
- craft sticks

Cost: $0.25
Price: $0.50
Profit: $0.25

To make the flowers, glue foam circles onto foam flower shapes. Glue flower heads onto colored craft sticks. Let dry.

Tip: *Use an egg carton and colored sand to show off your beautiful blossoms.*

Petal Pencils

You will need:
- heavy paper
- scissors
- craft foam
- pencils
- craft glue

Sketch a daisy shape onto heavy paper, cut it out, and use it as a pattern. Using the pattern as a guide, cut a daisy from craft foam for each pencil.

Fold the daisy in half and cut 2 slits into the center. Slip a pencil through the slits. Attach a foam circle to the center with craft glue. Let dry.

Tip: *Stick the pencils into a flat piece of green floral foam (available at craft and garden-supply stores).*

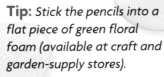

Cost: $0.50
Price: $1.00
Profit: $0.50

Summer Stand

Make the most of neighborhood garage sales by setting up a sale for your crafty creations.

Cat Grass

You will need:
- cat grass seeds
- soil
- water
- plastic cups

Grow cat grass (available at pet-supply stores) in colorful plastic cups. Follow the directions on the seed package for growing. It will take about one to two weeks for your cat grass to grow.

Cost: $0.50

Price: $1.00

Profit: $0.50

Tip: *Add a cute cat sticker to the front of each cup so that your customers know what the product is.*

Flashy Tacks

You will need:
- acrylic paint
- paintbrush
- flattened decorative glass marbles
- double-sided foam tape
- large, flat tacks

Cost: $0.50
Price: $1.00
Profit: $0.50

Paint simple designs on the bottoms of flattened decorative glass marbles (available at craft and flower stores). Let dry. Use double-sided foam tape to stick the marbles onto large, flat tacks.

Tip: *Use old corks or a small bulletin board to display your tacks and protect your customers from getting poked.*

Something Fishy

You will need:
- picture frame
- blue paper
- fish stickers
- bubble wrap
- double-sided tape

 Ask an adult to remove the glass from a picture frame and replace it with blue paper. Put stickers of fish and other undersea creatures on the paper. Attach a piece of bubble wrap with double-sided tape.

Cost: $3.00
Price: $6.00
Profit: $3.00

Tip: *Use craft paint to change the color of the frame.*

Clever Coasters

You will need:
- round cork coasters
- buttons
- craft glue

Glue buttons around the edges of round cork coasters (available at craft stores). Let dry.

Tip: *Sell cups of cold lemonade along with your coasters.*

Cost: $0.75
Price: $1.50
Profit: $0.75

Button Bugs

You will need:
- pipe cleaners
- scissors
- buttons
- glue
- googly eyes
- magnets

For each bug, carefully cut 2 inches off the end of a pipe cleaner. Slide the small pipe cleaner through the holes on a button. Glue on googly eyes. Glue the bug onto a magnet and let dry.

Tip: *Use your Button Bugs to hold a picture on an uncoated aluminum cookie sheet. Set the sheet on a frame stand.*

Cost: $0.25

Price: $0.50

Profit: $0.25

Fall Festival

The start of the school year and Halloween are the perfect times to cash in with cool autumn crafts.

Charm Books

You will need:
- colored paper
- scissors
- ¾-inch-tall cabinet hinges
- glue
- decorative items (such as beads, glitter, and stickers)
- white paper
- ruler
- thin ribbon

1. For each book, cut two pieces of colored paper to fit the front and back of a hinge (available at hardware stores). Glue in place. Decorate the cover with small decorative items. Let dry.

2. To make pages, cut a strip of white paper 4 inches long by ¾ inch wide. Fanfold the paper strip to fit inside the hinge. Open hinge. Glue ends of paper to inside of hinge. Let dry.

3. Poke a hole in the back cover through the top screw hole. Fold a 12-inch ribbon in half to make a loop. Thread the ribbon ends through the hole, then through the ribbon loop. Pull snug. Knot ends.

Tip: *Stick a flat tack through the back of each book and hang the charm books at eye level on a piece of cardboard.*

Cost: $2.50
Price: $5.00
Profit: $2.50

Spirit Scrunchies

You will need:
- fleece
- scissors
- hair elastics

Using fleece in your school colors, cut about 12 strips measuring 1 inch by 6 inches for each scrunchie. Tie fleece strips in knots around a hair elastic.

Tip: *Use an empty paper towel roll to display your scrunchies.*

Cost: $0.50
Price: $1.00
Profit: $0.50

Scream Rings

Tip: *Spread fake spiderwebs (available where Halloween decorations are sold) across your table and stick in your spiders.*

You will need:
- black pipe cleaners
- black buttons
- black cord
- black felt
- googly eyes

For each ring, carefully thread half of a black pipe cleaner through two holes of a button. Twist the ends of the pipe cleaner together to form a ring. Glue pieces of black cord to the button for legs. Cut a round piece of felt and glue it on top of the legs. Add googly eyes.

Cost: $0.25
Price: $0.50
Profit: $0.25

Going Batty

You will need:
- scissors
- felt
- glue
- plastic spoons
- double-sided tape
- lollipops
- ribbon
- googly eyes

Cost: $0.50
Price: $1.00
Profit: $0.50

1. Use scissors to cut felt wings and ears. Glue them to plastic spoons. Let dry.

2. Use double-sided tape to attach a lollipop to each spoon. Tie a ribbon around the lollipop stick and spoon to secure.

3. Glue googly eyes on the bat's face. Let dry.

Tip: *Make bats look like they're in flight by sticking them into a cone-shaped piece of styrofoam.*

Fuzzy Frames

For each frame, you will need:
- four craft sticks
- glue
- pom-poms
- adhesive magnets

Glue 4 craft sticks together to make a frame. Let dry. Squeeze glue onto the frame and attach pom-poms. Let dry. Stick magnets onto the back corners of the frame.

Tip: *On a sheet of paper that fits the frame, write "Your photo here." Attach it to the back of the frame with double-sided tape.*

Cost: $2.00

Price: $4.00

Profit: $2.00

Winter Bazaar

Use the holidays and snowy weather
to inspire craft ideas to sell as gifts.

Candy Cane Forest

You will need:
- felt
- pinking shears
- craft glue
- rhinestones, ribbons, confetti, and fabric paint
- wrapped candy canes

For each tree, fold a piece of felt in half and use pinking shears to cut a triangle shape. You will have two triangles that are the same size. Glue sides of tree together leaving the bottom open. Let dry. Decorate tree by gluing on rhinestones, ribbons, and confetti, and by doodling with dimensional fabric paint. Let dry and slip in a candy cane.

Tip: *Place candy canes into a piece of white styrofoam to look like a forest standing in the snow.*

Cost: $1.00

Price: $2.00

Profit: $1.00

Nifty Gifts

You will need:
- Mod Podge
- small wooden squares
- wrapping paper
- scissors
- craft glue
- magnets
- mini bows

To make these magnets, brush Mod Podge onto the top of wooden squares. Stick the squares onto the back of festive wrapping paper. Let dry. Trim excess paper. Glue magnets to the backs. Let dry. Stick a mini bow on top of each square.

Cost: $0.50

Price: $1.00

Profit: $0.50

Tip: *Place gift magnets on a clean metal cookie pan. Prop pan up so that customers can see their choices.*

Snowflake Charms

You will need:
- craft glue
- confetti snowflakes
- metal-rimmed tags
- rhinestones
- dimensional fabric paint
- ribbon

Use glue to attach confetti snowflakes onto metal-rimmed tags (available at scrapbook and office-supply stores). Glue a rhinestone to the center of each tag using a dot of dimensional fabric paint. Let dry. Thread the tag onto a ribbon to make a cool necklace.

Tip: *Put a charm on a key ring and sell as a key chain or luggage tag.*

Cost: $0.25
Price: $0.50
Profit: $0.25

Pencil Toppers

You will need:

- scissors
- felt
- craft glue
- pencils
- confetti snowflakes
- rhinestones

For each pencil, cut a thin strip of felt 4 inches long. Squeeze a line of glue along the felt strip. Roll the felt around the pencil. Hold firmly for about one minute. Set aside and let dry. Attach a confetti snowflake and a rhinestone with glue. Let dry.

Cost: $0.50
Price: $1.00
Profit: $0.50

Tip: *Put your pencils into a clean empty soup can covered with decorative felt trees.*

Photo Clips

You will need:
- acrylic paint
- sponge paintbrush
- pre-cut wooden shapes
- wooden clothespins
- craft glue
- rhinestones

Paint wooden shapes and clothespins with acrylic paint. Glue the shapes onto the clothespins so that they stand upright. Let dry. Decorate with rhinestones.

Cost: $1.00
Price: $2.00
Profit: $1.00

Tip: *Put a photo into a clip so that customers can see how the clip works.*

Sierra

"I think the Bitty Bobbies are cute hair accessories. I sold them for $0.50 each and made $5."
-Sierra

Hanna

"I sold 20 Charm Books at my school store. Everyone thought they were really cute."
-Hanna

"I thought making the Garden Greetings was a lot of fun!"
        -Lauren

Made with 💗 by
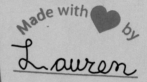
Lauren

Tell us all about what you sold at your craft sale!

Craft Sale Editor
American Girl
8400 Fairway Place
Middleton, WI 53562

Did you like these crafts?
Find lots more in *American Girl* magazine!

American Girl is the most popular magazine in
the country published exclusively for girls! It's packed with
fiction, games, puzzles, crafts, recipes, advice, party plans,
special surprises, and more!

Try it risk-free!

Simply mail this card today

Mail this card to receive a **risk-free** preview issue and start your one-year subscription. For just $22.95, you'll receive 6 bimonthly issues! If you don't love *American Girl*® right away, just write "cancel" on your invoice. The preview issue is yours to keep, free.

The magazine especially for girls 8 and up

☐ 1 year (6 issues) $22.95

Send bill to: (please print)

Adult's name

Address

City   State   Zip

Adult's signature

Send magazine to: (please print)

Girl's name   Birth date *(optional)*

Address

City   State   Zip

Guarantee: You may cancel at any time for a full refund on all unserved issues. Allow 4-6 weeks for first issue.
Non-U.S. subscriptions $29 U.S., prepaid only. © 2008 American Girl, LLC.

K8lAGL

Request a FREE catalogue!

Books are just the beginning...

Discover dolls, clothing, furniture, and accessories that inspire girls to imagine their own stories.

Just mail this card, call 1-800-845-0005, or visit americangirl.com.

Parent's name   /   /   Girl's birth date

Address

City   State   Zip

Parent's e-mail *(provide to receive updates, and Web-exclusive offers)*

(   )
Parent's phone   ☐ Home ☐ Work

Parent's signature   12583i

Send a catalogue to a grandparent or a friend:

Name

Address

City   State   Zip

☐ Grandparent 15262li   ☐ Friend 12591i

Today's Date

Visit americangirl.com
and click on **Fun for Girls**
for quizzes and games.

|| |||

Place
Stamp
Here

 American Girl®
PO BOX 620497
MIDDLETON WI 53562-0497

Iıldıııılldıldıldıııldlllıııldldlıldııılldıdıııldlldı